ISBN Paperback: 978-1068612251
ISBN Hardback: 978-1068612268

Text and Illustrations by Siski Kalla
Design Audrey Sauble
Published by Catch a Leaf Publishing

JNF037020 JUVENILE NONFICTION / Science & Nature / Environmental Conservation & Protection
NAT045000 NATURE / Ecosystems & Habtitats / General
JNF003170 JUVENILE NONFICTION / Animals / Pets
JNF051000 JUVENILE NONFICTION / Science & Nature / General

First Edition, 2024

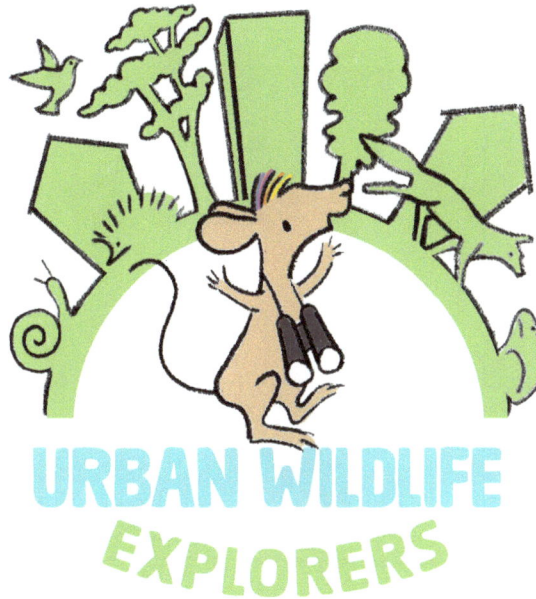

URBAN WILDLIFE EXPLORERS

To all the children growing up in towns and cities who love nature.

To all the children who'll move a snail off the path, scoop a ladybird out of water, and gently capture a moth to release it outside.

To all the children who care about wildlife – you are amazing!

Today let's explore
SNAILS!

Can you
answer this
question for me?

What makes a snail a snail?

What makes a snail a snail?

A snail has a shell!

A **slug**, which is similar, doesn't.
So one thing that makes a snail is its **shell**.

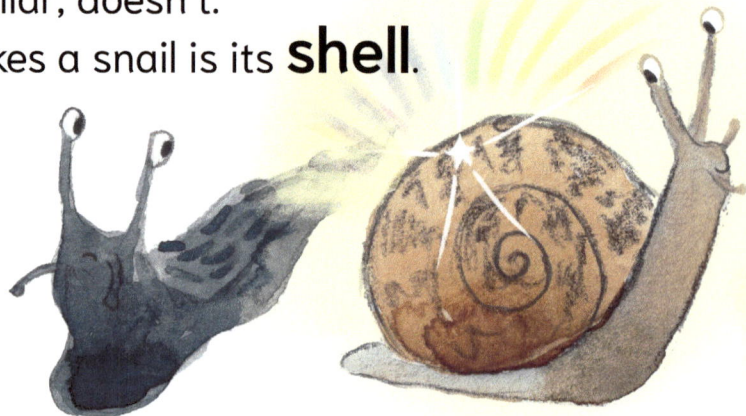

When a snail is in **danger**, it will **hide** in its shell.

Can you protect yourself with a shell?
Maybe you already do?

Can you curl up inside a small space like a snail?

It's dark
in here!

A snail makes its own **shell** (a bit like we make our own hair and fingernails!). It grows bigger and bigger as the snail grows. Most snail shells coil to the right (clockwise) but you might be lucky to spot one that coils the other way!

Someone
drew on me!

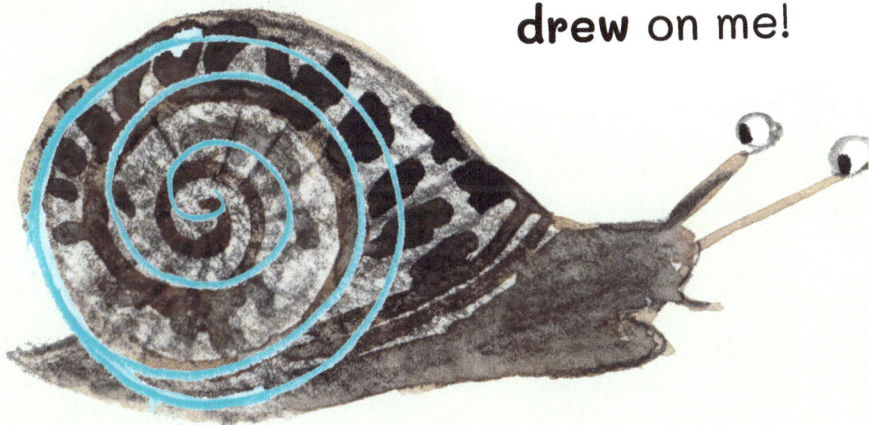

Snails have a shell to protect their soft bodies. They don't have bones!

I don't have bones, or ears, or eyes! But I can feel it when you walk on the ground above me!'

We don't have bones either!

When animals don't have a backbone, they are called **invertebrates**. Some examples of invertebrates are snails, slugs, worms, caterpillars and butterflies, ants, spiders, beetles, jellyfish, crabs and lobsters, too!

Like snails, these animals don't have any bones at all!

To protect themselves from other animals they have:

Shells (snails), or
a carapace (crabs, lobsters);

Colour/pattern that either makes it easier to hide (camouflage) or bright colours as a warning 'not to eat' (caterpillars and butterflies, grasshoppers, spiders, and some species of snail, too);

When they are threatened, shield bugs and ladybirds release horrible **smells**.

What else makes a snail a snail?

They are very, very slow. So slow...

SO slow...

...that it would take a Common Garden Snail at least 6 minutes to cross four pages in this book. They can move at up to 2.4mm per second! The muscles in the snail's body that helps move it forward are in its 'foot'.
Unlike you, a snail only has one foot!

Nearly there!

Being slow can help protect snails against predators, as many **predators** – birds, for example – use movement to spot prey.

How far can a snail go?

They can get quite far!

A common garden snail might move more than 20 metres in a day/night (24 hours) if the ground is moist.

A snail can remember its 'home' and will travel back once it has been exploring.

How many tentacles do I have? None! These are actually called my 'arms'.

What makes a snail a snail?

A snail has tentacles.

The top tentacles have eyes; the lower pair are for tasting and feeling. Both pairs help snails 'smell' their way to food.

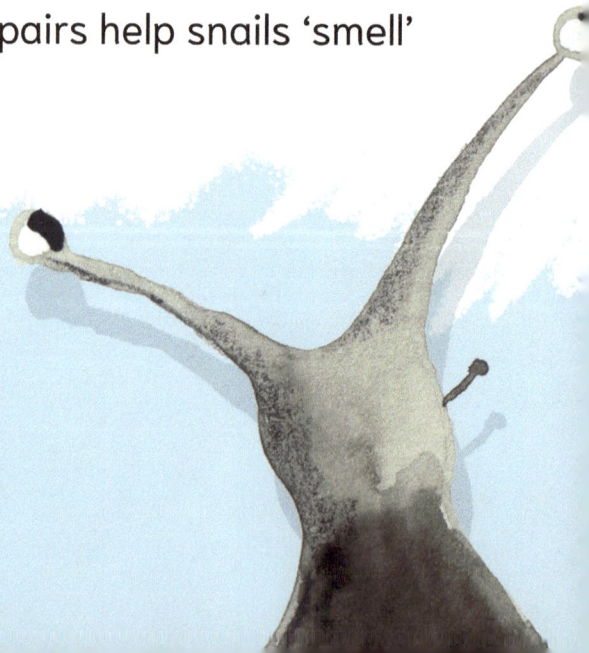

Imagine if you had your eyeballs on tentacles at the top of your head!

Your eyes are protected by your bones, eyelashes, eyelids, and you can also cover your eyes with your hands. A snail doesn't have eyelashes – wouldn't that look funny? – or hands, or bones. So it protects itself by pulling the tentacles in.

Funny?!
How rude!

What makes a snail a snail?

Snails are SLIMY and SLIPPERY!

Why are snails slimy underneath? So they can move more easily.

Rub your hands together. Now put some hand lotion on your hands and try again. It's much easier with the lotion! The snail's slippery **mucous** is like the lotion – it helps it move.

The slime also helps the
snail 'stick' to things, like
windows, walls or plant pots.

What makes a snail a snail?

Snails lay eggs!

A snail such as the common garden snail might lay 80 eggs near a plant that baby snails love to eat. Snails love hostas, a plant that a lot of gardeners also love.

My poor hostas!

My babies will be safe here!

Most snails eat plants, fresh or rotting. They are herbivorous. Some species are **omnivorous** though – that means they eat plants and animals. Although they'll usually only eat something that's already dead.

Snails have thousands of tiny teeth, on a tongue-like structure called the radula. It's like sandpaper on a nail file, it rips and scrapes the food so it can be eaten.

What else do we know about snails?

They're in trouble!

help

Worldwide, many species of snail are at risk of extinction. Hotter, drier weather makes life hard. **Malacologists**, scientists who study molluscs including snails, work to understand how we can help protect them.

Habitat loss caused by building in green areas, cutting grass and weeds, and lack of water add to the threat to all invertebrate life, including snails.

You
can
help
snails!

Possibly the biggest threat to snails is climate change – if they can't adapt to different weather conditions (less rain, or more heat, or more extreme weather and storms) they won't survive. Luckily, there are things you can do to help!

Snail rescue!

You might find a snail that needs help. Maybe it's in the middle of a road, or far from plants and moisture. If it's already hiding in its shell, you can move it somewhere cool, moist and dark. If it's still moving, you can tap it gently on its shell to encourage it to go inside its shell. Do not try to lift a snail unless it's inside its shell, as you can injure it!

Just don't call me Shellie.

You can bring a snail indoors for a while. Some people keep snails as pets.

You'll need:

- a large container with small air/ moisture holes
- natural soil, moss, twigs, leaves
- a mist sprayer to keep things damp
- keep in a place that doesn't have direct sunlight.

WASH your hands before and after handling snails!

Look out for:

A snail breathing. The breathing pore (called a pneumostome) is like a hole in the side of the snail just tucked under the shell edge. A snail using its feelers to explore.

Listen out for:

A snail eating. You can hear it if you're quiet!
A snail moving up the side of the container – watch how its foot muscle ripples as it moves.

Yum!
Lettuce eat!

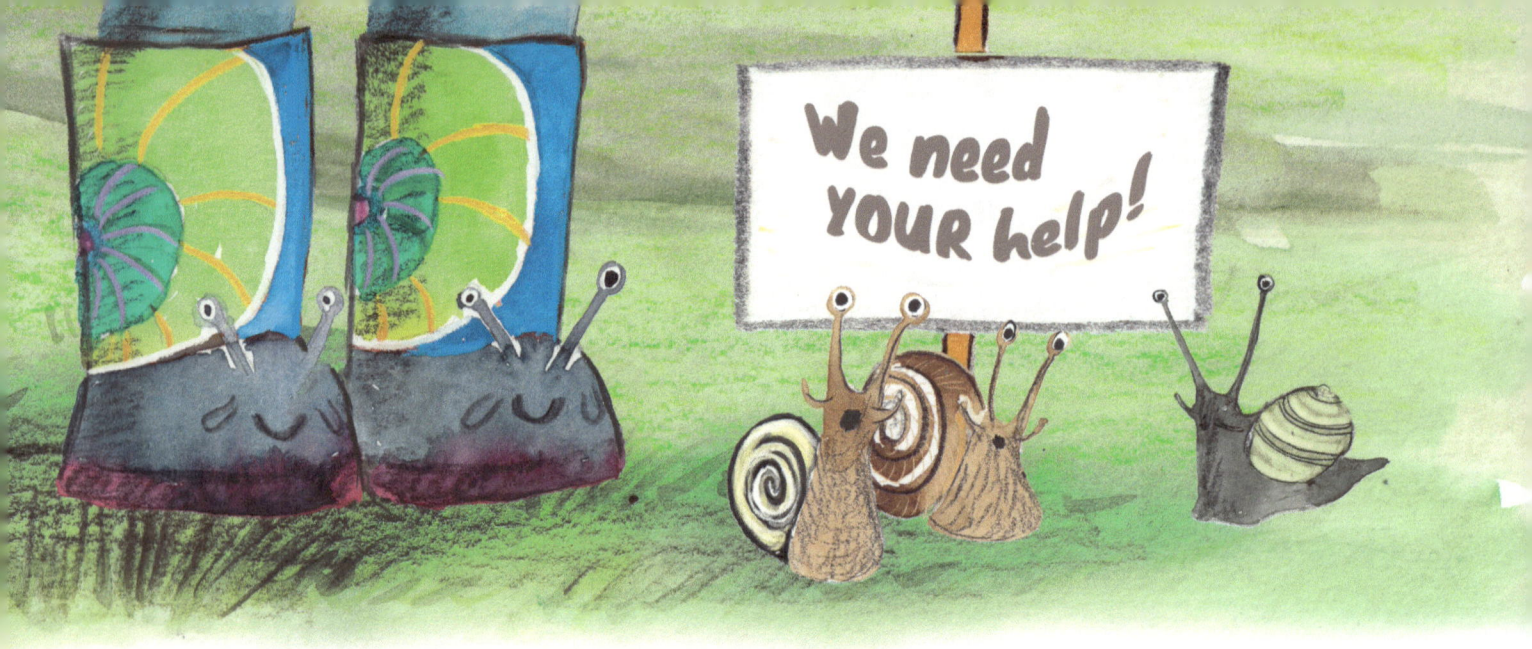

How can you protect snails and other invertebrates?

Snails and other animals can't tell us what they need, but there are some things we know will help **protect** them.

Reuse and recycle

Create wildlife havens

Use solar power instead of fossil fuels

Volunteer!

Ask your parents to join litter clean-up days, do bird, butterfly or biodiversity counts, join local wildlife groups. Check Earthwatch Europe (online) to find out about tree planting or other earth-friendly activities in your area.

Write to your MP or local councillor

Ask them to consider banning insecticides and molluscicides from local parks and natural areas.

Talk to your school

You can also ask your school to leave some areas safe for snails, as well as join in on biodversity counts.

No to pesticides!

Choose plants that snails don't like (ferns, rosemary, lavendar, azaleas). Provide a compost or logs away from special plants, too.

Do you want to see snails?

Snails are more active at night or in damp weather. Look under plant leaves, pots, planks of wood, and near fences.

Can you find traces of snails? Use a torch to shine a light around your front door or nearby, and it'll be easier to spot their silvery **trails**.

Where do snails go when it's cold?
Snails hibernate.

A snail will **burrow** into the soil, under a log or a plant pot. A snail makes a special cover for the entrance of the shell to protect itself, and it will 'sleep' until it gets warmer.

What do you do differently in winter?

Keep it down! Trying to sleep here!

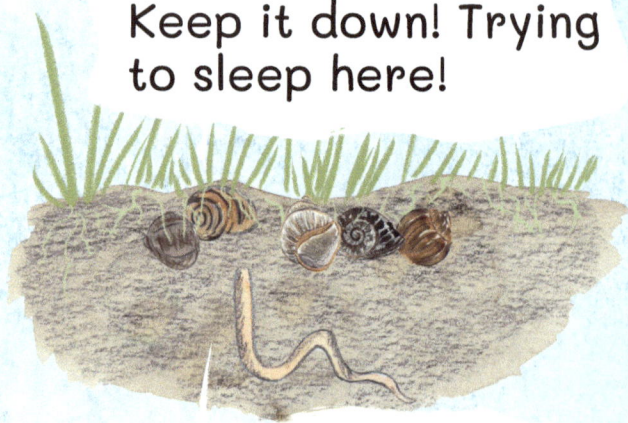

Oi! This is my home!

Turn a plant pot upside down and you might find lots of snails all together like this!

They also make the same **epiphragm** (cover over the shell entrance) when it's too hot and dry. They hide in their shells and won't go out to feed until it gets cooler and wetter again.

When it's too hot, I stay in the shade. Sometimes I use a fan!

Pots are lovely — dark, cool and damp. Under bricks, too. But pots with seedlings are my favourite!

I also eat rubbish!

Why are snails important?
Because they eat rubbish!

Snails eat things we wouldn't want to! They help **recycle** and 'move' nutrients from plants into and through the soil, making it healthier and better for growing plants.

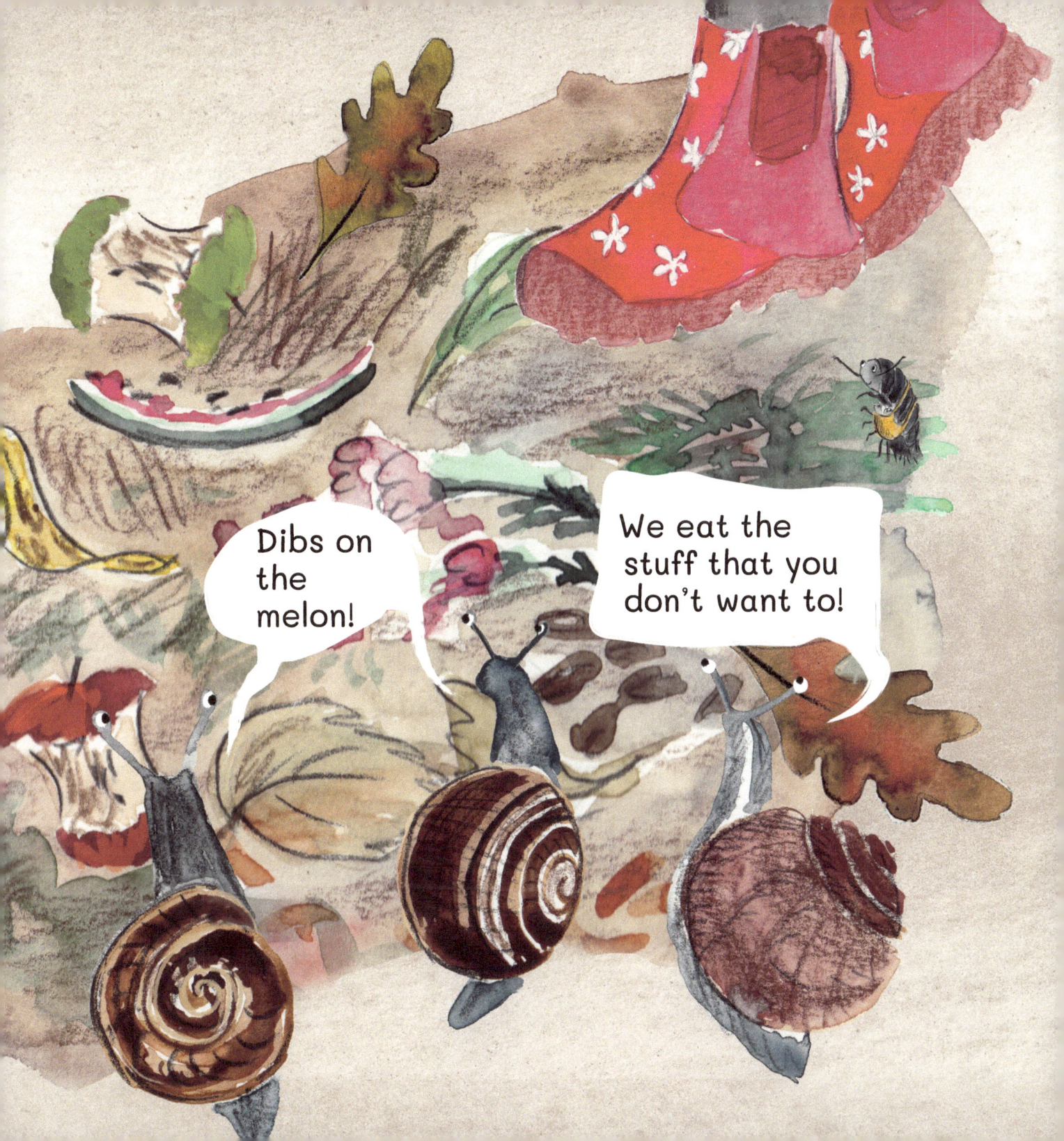

Snails in the food web

Lots of things eat snails – so they can be important part of diet for other animals. Some animals like the glow worm beetle completely rely on eating snails and slugs to survive!

Snail poo is a great **fertiliser** – it makes soil even better for plants to grow!

We are unique!

Even two snails of the same species aren't exactly the same. Look at the shells of two common garden snails, for example, and you'll see small differences in the shell **patterns**.

My shell is the most beautiful!

As if!

If I were a snail, I might look like this!

I'm not a real snail. I am imaginary!

I'm a brown-lipped snail, from Europe. I can be brown, pink, yellow or even white!

We live in Cuba!

I'm African! I'm also VERY big!

I prefer cheese!

Some snails are edible. But that doesn't mean you can eat them straight off a plant pot! They may have bacteria or parasites that can make you very sick.

In places where snails are eaten, such as France, they are given a special diet to 'clean out' their bodies first.

Let's make a snail that rocks!
An easy and fun way to make your own pet snail!

Art recipe ingredients:

thick coloured paper

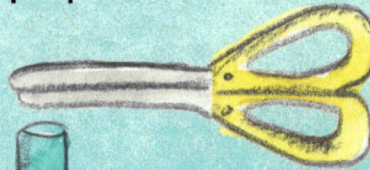

scissors

glue

colouring pens

a bowl or other circular
object to trace around

1) Cut out a large circle.

2) Fold in the middle. It should look like this

3) Cut out the 'head' of the snail.

4) Colour some eyes.

5) Glue to the back of your folded circle.

6) Now cut a slightly smaller circle to colour or cut out various sizes and glue them on top of each other. Have fun!

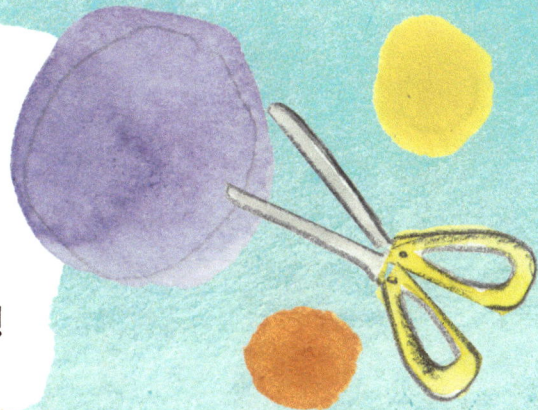

earthwatch
EUROPE

Earthwatch Europe

Every purchase of this book is a positive change for our planet. For every sale of this book 50p goes to support Earthwatch Europe, an environmental charity with science at its heart.

Earthwatch works to create a world where we live in balance with nature by helping people to protect the nature around them. Earthwatch builds meaningful nature connections and gives people the tools they need to fight for our planet. Working alongside communities and organisations, Earthwatch builds an understanding and a love of nature, and help everyone to protect the natural world. Guided by science and powered by people, Earthwatch creates change through connection.

Find out more at Earthwatch.org.uk

Some other great organisations

Canal & River Trust This non-profit is focused on the UK's waterways, with lots of opportunities to get involved. Learn more here: canalrivertrust.org.uk

The Wildlife Trusts There are 46 Wildlife Trusts in the UK, go to www.wildlifetrusts.org to find one local to you.

Buglife Buglife is the only organisation in Europe devoted to the conservation of all invertebrates. Go to www.buglife.org.uk for more information.

URBAN WILDLIFE EXPLORERS

For more information about books in the Urban Wildlife Explorers series and to learn more about our urban wildlife, head to www.urbanwildlifeexplorers.com

Look out for these things hiding in each book!

Siski Kalla, author and illustrator of *Let's Explore Snails!*
Visit her website www.siskikallaillustration.com to download activity sheets and more!

I grew up in London and really wanted to find children's books about wildlife there. There weren't any. So I decided to make the books that 'child me' would have loved. I'm not a scientist though so I got some help! For this book a malacologist made sure the facts were correct. And I did get things wrong. I didn't know that almost all snails' shells coil to the right, for example. I had drawn lots of snails coiling to the left when in reality that's rare!

Everyone wears it this way!

Nah mate, yer shell's on back to front!

www.ingramcontent.com/pod-product-compliance
Lightning Source LLC
Chambersburg PA
CBHW060856270326
41934CB00003B/171